BUGS THAT GO BLAM!

AND OTHER CREEPY-CRAWLER TRIVIA

by Barbara Seuling

illustrated by Tim Davis

Willowisp Press

This book is for Philip Richard Antonelli

Published by Willowisp Press
801 94th Avenue North, St. Petersburg, Florida 33702

Text copyright © 1995 by Barbara Seuling

Illustrations copyright © 1995 by Willowisp Press,
a division of PAGES, Inc.

Printed in the United States of America

2 4 6 8 10 9 7 5 3 1

ISBN 0-87406-774-X

CONTENTS

A WORD ABOUT BUGS

Not everything that is called a bug *is* a bug. I think it's only fair to warn you: The term "bug" only applies, technically, to an insect with a beak that pierces its victim. I use the word bug, however, as a lot of people do—to describe the tiny creatures that crawl, creep, fly, wiggle, and hop through our gardens, homes, and backyards, as well as through meadows, forests, and jungles of the world.

Experts have spent their lives classifying all the members of the animal kingdom into neat divisions called Classes, Orders, Families, and Species. This makes it a lot easier for those who want to identify a creature or look it up for further study, so I have included the name of the Order to which each creature belongs. Still, with all due respect to science authorities, I'll continue to refer to these creatures the old-fashioned way, and hope this will not bug too many people.

—Barbara Seuling

IT'S A
SMALL &
WACKY
WORLD

✺ Although scientists have identified more than a million species of insects, the actual number is probably so big it would be hard to imagine. Some experts say there are 200 million insects for every human on earth. And that figure doesn't count spiders, centipedes, and worms!

✺ Seven thousand new insect species are discovered each year.

🐜 There are ways to tell whether a bug is an insect or not. Insects have three body segments—the head, thorax, and abdomen. Spiders are not insects because they have only two body segments. Centipedes are not insects because they can have many segments.

🐜 Another way to tell bugs apart is by the number of legs. Insects have six legs. Spiders have eight. Centipedes can have more than a hundred! And worms have no legs at all.

🐜 Some insects, such as crickets and grasshoppers, have ears on their front legs.

✷ The blood of insects is colorless or pale yellow. The red blood you might see in a squashed insect came from some other animal.

✷ Insects are eaten in many parts of the world. Cockroaches have been used as a gourmet seasoning. In China, silkworms are eaten as a delicacy. The ancient Greeks

and Romans snacked on beetle larvae. American Indians in the early days of the West roasted crickets and grasshoppers or made them into soup. Honey ants are like candy to some natives of Australia, Central America, and Mexico.

✳ The Algonquin Indians grouped insects together based on the creatures' desire to bite people. Together, the mosquito, blackfly, and biting midge were called "sawgimay," which roughly means "small-person-who-flies-and-bites-so-fiercely."

✳ Half of all insects eat other insects.

✳ Most of the insects in the rain forests live way up in the tops of trees and never touch the ground.

✳ Some insect fossils date back 40 million years.

Insects are millions of years ahead of humans in many things. They were the first to fly and to use solar navigation—finding their way by the sun. They constructed homes out of wood, clay, and earth long before humans did. They kept gardens and livestock and cultivated food crops. They sewed, made paper, landscaped the ground around their homes, and used air conditioning. They set up communication systems, divided their work load, and built nurseries. They also formed armies, went to war, and kept slaves.

* If you're not moving around too much, insect repellent can protect your face even if you put it on your ankles. That's because a column of air currents rises around your body from the ground and carries the repellent upward.

* Humans have never been able to exterminate a single insect species.

* Several species of insects are imported by gardeners to get rid of other insects. Ladybugs and praying mantises are popular among gardeners. Soldier bugs, which eat more than 100 kinds of destructive garden pests, are also favorites.

ANTS, WASPS, & BEES

ORDER: HYMENOPTERA

 Ants, wasps, and bees are closely related. They are considered the most intelligent of insects with the most highly developed social life.

 Almost every other insect is an orphan because it will never know its parents. Only bees, wasps, ants, and termites take care of their families. Most female insects die soon after they lay their eggs.

✳ In proportion to their size, ants have the largest brains of any animal in the animal kingdom.

✳ There are more than 3,500 known species of ants.

✳ In the Amazon rain forest of Peru, one entomologist from the Smithsonian Institution found forty-three different kinds of ants living in just one tree.

✳ Members of an ant colony know each other by their special odor, or *pheromones*. They use this scent to let other ants know where they can find food, or to attract a mate, or to call for help in removing a dead ant from the nest. An ant with an unfamiliar odor is considered a stranger.

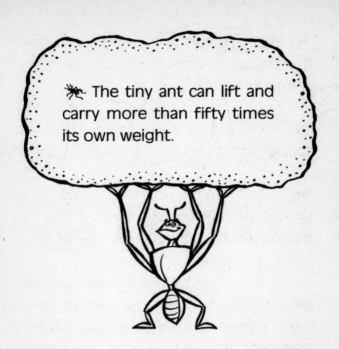

The tiny ant can lift and carry more than fifty times its own weight.

Fire ants sting their victims. Then, using their bodies as "squirt guns," they spray burning liquid into the wound.

Hunting ants are used as insect traps by farmers in the tropics. A nest of the ants is placed in a tree. The hunting ants clean out every other insect. Then the farmer moves the nest to the next tree. Whole orchards are kept free of harmful insects this way.

In Africa and South America, army ants move through the jungle like a living carpet. They attack wasps' nests fearlessly. Even jungle cats and snakes flee from them.

Army ants live up to their name. They march every day, stopping to rest each night. They only settle down long enough for the queen to lay eggs, and then they move on again. When they have to move over a large open area, they form a bridge with their own bodies, each army ant hanging on to the next one. At night, they use their bodies

to create a "hanging hotel" that even has passageways and individual rooms.

※ Harvester ants raid the warehouses of other harvester ants to steal their food supply—seeds.

※ Ants have cleaning hooks on their front legs. They use them to clean their antennae.

※ When a soldier parasol ant bites, it never lets go. Some Honduran Indians use these inch-long ants to close up wounds. The Indians hold the skin together on both sides of the wound and place an ant over it. The ant bites and its jaws lock, holding the skin together. If the wound is large, several ants are used. Once the jaws lock, the bodies of the ants are pulled off, leaving the heads in place like staples.

Tailor or weaver ants sew the edges of two leaves together to make a nest. For a needle, they use their own larvae, pushed in and out. The thread is silk released by the larvae.

Some ants keep tiny insect "cattle"—aphids—that they "milk" for droplets of nectar. They even build little cow sheds for their cattle out of earth or of paper made from chewed fibers.

✺ Honey ants use certain members of their colony as living storage tanks. These ants swell with nectar, looking like yellow marbles. They can hardly move. If they are fed too much, they can explode. When the colony cannot find other food, the storage ants regurgitate, and the rest of the ants eat the nectar that has been saved for this moment.

✺ Most full-grown insects have wings and can fly at some point in their lives.

After an ant queen goes on her wedding flight and mates, she drops to earth and chews off her wings. She spends the rest of her life in darkness, doing nothing but eating and laying eggs.

🐜 Bees build their hives of wax, which comes from their bodies. Each cell in a hive has six sides. This hexagonal shape makes the best use of space and requires a minimal amount of bee wax.

🐜 Beehive cells are so precise—half an inch long and a quarter of an inch wide—that a scientist once suggested that cells be used as a unit of measurement.

🐝 There is a kind of air conditioning in a beehive. The bees fan their wings when it is hot, sending a cool flow of air through the hive. If it is extremely hot, the bees place diluted honey or water at the openings of empty cells, which evaporates and cools the air as it is fanned.

🐝 The honeycombs of giant bees in India can be 7 feet tall and weigh as much as 400 pounds.

🐝 Honeybees use honey to defend themselves. An unwanted visitor might be drenched in honey so that he cannot fight, forcing him to leave. If a large

intruder, such as a mouse, accidentally stumbles into a hive, it is stung to death and covered with a sticky material that comes from twigs and buds. The coating dries like a shell, leaving the creature inside its own tomb within the hive.

🐝 When a bee stings a mammal, it cannot remove its stinger from the victim, and it dies. When it stings another insect, it can use its stinger again.

🐝 More people die each year from bee stings than from snake bites.

※ There is never more than one queen bee in a hive. When an old queen leaves or dies, and a new queen comes out of her cocoon, she immediately uses her stinger to stab all her sisters to death.

※ On a sunny day, the queen bee goes on the only flight of her life. As part of the mating ritual, she leaves the hive and flies upward, as male bees follow. Those who can't keep up with her drop dead from exhaustion.

※ The act of mating for bees is so violent that it shatters the male's body and tears him apart.

🐝 For many centuries, people believed that the largest member of a bee hive was a king bee. It was not until 1609 that scientists discovered that the dominant bee was a queen bee.

🐝 Male bees are born for only one purpose—to mate with the queen. They cannot eat on their own and are at the mercy of the female bees to feed them. They have no stingers and cannot defend themselves. They are the first to be thrown out of the hive when honey is scarce. After mating, the males die, and those that fail in mating are cast out of the hive.

🐝 The queen bee is continually pampered. She is massaged by worker bees and fed a rich diet of royal jelly, a mixture that comes from nurse bees. She does nothing but eat and lay eggs—sometimes 3,000 a day—for life.

🐜 In the first hour after a bee baby is born, it is fed about five hundred times.

🐜 There may be 80,000 bees in one hive, but only the queen can be a mother. All the other females are workers.

🐜 Worker bees do chores according to their age. The youngest, up to 4 days old, do housecleaning and babysit the eggs. When they are a little older, 4 to 12 days old, they feed the infant bees. From 12 to 21 days, they make repairs to the hive. When they are 21 days old, they go out and look for food. They live from 6 to 8 weeks and work until their wings are so tattered that the bees simply drop from exhaustion.

✳ In one day, a worker bee can gather half its own weight in pollen.

✳ Bees do a "waggle dance" when they find a good food supply. A bee dances in a figure eight. Based on how fast she moves and the angle of the dance, other bees learn where the food is and how to get to it.

🐝 Scientists can measure the amount of pollution in the atmosphere by studying bee pollen.

🐝 Bees collect pollen and carry it back to the hive on the hairs on their legs.

🐝 After the 1980 eruption of the Mount St. Helens volcano in the state of Washington, millions of bees died. Ash from the volcano got caught in the bees' hairs, and some bees could not get off the ground with all that extra weight. Those who did fly had nowhere to store pollen because ash had coated the leg hairs where the pollen is normally collected.

※ When bumblebees are caught in a shower, they take shelter in a hanging flower, using it like an umbrella.

※ Bees always find their way back to their hive by the position of the sun.

※ A bee may fly 60 miles a day while collecting food.

※ Once a bee visits a certain type of flower, such as a rose, it stays with that species until there is no nectar or pollen left. Then it will visit another type of flower.

🐜 There are bees in South America that will get "nectar" from old molasses cans, fruit peels, or even motor oil cans if they run out of flowers.

🐜 There are little wingless flies that hitchhike on the backs of bees, using them as airplanes. The travelers go back to the hive with the bees and lay eggs there. The eggs hatch, and the larvae help themselves to the food they find in the hive. When they are old enough to leave, they board another flight out of the hive.

✸ Not all bees live in hives. One type of European bee makes its nest in the abandoned shells of snails. The **Megachile** bee snips petals from flowers and rolls them into tubes, which serve as baby bee cradles. Plasterer bees live in underground burrows lined with a waxy substance.

✸ The bee **Colletes** makes its nest underground. When it lays an egg, it makes a little polyester bag, like a miniature plastic sandwich bag, with excretions from a special gland. The little bag has a loose flap at the top. The bee puts a supply of food in the bag and lays her egg in it. Then she seals the flap, keeping the offspring dry and safe from fungus infections. Chemists say that the polyester secreted by Colletes is no different from the polyester found in a tie or suit jacket, except that it is not woven.

🐜 The tiny carpenter bee builds an apartment house for her babies. She bores a long tunnel inside a broken twig, about 8 or 10 inches deep. (That's like a man digging a tunnel 200 feet deep with his bare hands.) She packs the bottom with pollen, lays an egg on top, and covers it with a partition. She repeats the process several times. The result is several little "apartments," each one housing an egg. When the eggs hatch, they eat the pollen, grow, and then chew their way out.

🐝 The Indians called honeybees "white man's flies."

🐝 Humans have never been able to make honey. Only bees can make it, and the process is still a mystery.

🐝 Unlike honeybees, wasps cannot produce wax. But some wasps make paper and build their nests out of it.

🐝 To make paper, wasps chew wood into little bits and mix it with their saliva. They spread the mixture out in thin sheets. These sheets are shaped into a nest a foot or more in diameter. The walls may have fifteen layers of paper. The paper is so fine it can be typed or written upon.

🐝 If a wasp chews wood from a red barn, its paper will come out with red streaks in it.

🐝 When it gets hot, worker wasps fly to a stream and collect water. They return and spit the water on the outside walls of the paper nest. As the water evaporates, it cools the inside of the nest.

🐜 Sawflies, a type of wasp, have a kind of saw blade on their tail section. They use it to saw through plant tissue.

🐜 The potter wasp makes a little mud pot for each egg she lays. Then she collects a supply of juicy caterpillars, stings them so they are still alive but paralyzed,  and stuffs them into the pot. She lays her egg inside and corks the pot. When the wasp egg hatches, the little larva feeds on the caterpillars until it is grown. Then it chews its way out from a hole in the side of the pot.

🐝 Each egg has its own little pot. It takes a potter wasp two to three hours to build each one. She works alone. Somehow, she knows whether an egg will produce a male or a female. For males, she builds smaller pots and stocks them with less food.

🐝 The enemy of the potter wasp is the tachina fly. When the wasp leaves the nest, the fly goes in and lays its own eggs. The fly eggs hatch immediately, and the larvae eat the caterpillars as well as the wasp's egg.

🐝 Seed and gall wasps are the only insects that can pollinate fig trees. Otherwise, the trees could not bear fruit. Fig growers even import seed and gall wasps for their orchards.

✳ Hunter wasps catch and paralyze spiders. The mud dauber, or *Tryposyloninae*, builds a mud house with many rooms, or cells. With its stinger it paralyzes spiders and puts one in each cell. Eggs are laid on top of the spiders, and when they hatch, the larvae eat the spiders. Sand wasps do the same thing with caterpillars.

✳ Hornets are members of the wasp family that live in colonies. Cows may walk close to hornet nests so that the hornets will eat the flies that are buzzing around the cows. The hornets pick off the flies but leave the cows alone.

🐜 Some wasps are so tiny that one could fit on the head of a pin.

🐜 Ichneumon wasps drill holes in trees, looking for wood-boring beetles. Some wasps get stuck in the holes, unable to remove their drills.

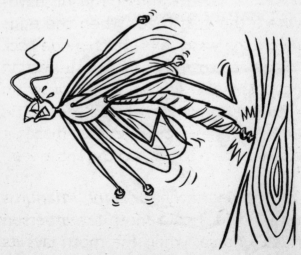

🕷 One wasp drags its victim, the fisher spider, along the surface of the water. It is easier to drag the weight over water than over other types of surfaces.

🕷 Wasps have their own "recycling squad" to get rid of leftovers from their meals. After they suck out the insides of their victims, they leave the remains to other insects, such as the larvae of the clothes moth. Those other insects feast on the empty skins.

🕷 The *Orasema* wasp loves fire ant larvae, so it lays its eggs on plant leaves where the ants feed. When the eggs hatch, the wasp larvae hitch a ride back to the ant colony on the unsuspecting ants. There, the wasp larvae grow up with the odor of the ants' nest. The odor provides a disguise that makes it easy for them to prey on the ant larvae.

🕷 Another hitchhiker is the *Phanurus* wasp. It rides on a moth like a person rides a horse. When the moth lays its eggs, the wasp gets off and lays her own eggs on top of the moth's. The wasp larvae eat the moth larvae, so only the wasps survive.

🐜 Wasps can get drunk. They have been known to drink fermenting juice until they pass out.

BEETLES
ORDER: COLEOPTERA

🐜 There are more beetles than anything else in the animal kingdom. One out of every five known species of living creatures is a species of beetle.

🐜 Some wood-boring beetles knock their heads against the walls of their tunnels—often a dead log—when they are disturbed. This can make the log sound like it's ticking.

🐜 Desert beetles have such a bad smell that when other insects are put in the same container with them, the other insects can die from the fumes. Even the beetles giving off the bad smell can drop dead.

🐜 Click beetles fling themselves into the air when they are threatened. This surprising behavior usually sends the attacker running.

🐜 In 1479, the larvae of click beetles, called wireworms, were tried and found guilty of destroying crops—and then expelled from the church by the bishop of Lausanne, Switzerland. But when crops continued to be ruined by the wireworms, the bishop declared a mistrial. He said the verdict was invalid because no friendly witnesses—like the birds that eat wireworms—had been called to testify in their defense.

🐜 Burying beetles, also known as burrowing or sexton beetles, collect insect corpses as food for their young. They dig a hole under the corpse and let it fall in. Then they cover it with fresh earth, making a little grave. Under the ground, the beetle babies, or grubs, feast on the decaying corpse.

🐜 The bombardier beetle, only half an inch long, can eject "bombs" of deadly chemicals at its enemy. It fires the bombs from its rear end with a loud "pop." Each explosion releases a deadly mixture of gases. The bombardier beetle can "fire" up to six times.

✷ The drugstore beetle got its name from its amazing ability to eat more than forty-five different substances, including aconite and belladonna, which are poisons.

✷ The **Oncideres** beetle keeps the mimosa tree healthy. It makes a slit in a tree limb and lays its eggs in it. The larvae cannot eat live wood, so the adult beetle strips the bark around the limb. That kills the branch and it falls to the ground, where the larvae can grow. A pruned mimosa tree lives about four times as long as one that has not been pruned.

🐜 If the oil of the blister beetle comes in contact with human skin, it can cause a blister. But when the oil is mixed one part per thousand in a solution, it has been found to help hair grow.

🐜 One type of beetle uses the water lily pad as a floating airfield. After it lands, it cuts a small hole through the leaf, pushes its abdomen into the water below, and lays its eggs. The eggs cling to the underside of the pad while the beetle stays nice and dry on top.

🐜 Fireflies and glowworms are neither flies nor worms. They are beetles.

🐜 The "light" you see on fireflies comes from a substance called *luciferin*. It glows, but it does not produce much light.

🐜 It's a mystery why a whole field full of fireflies often lights up at the same time. Nobody can explain how fireflies know exactly when to turn their lights on.

🐜 Male fireflies give off a light to attract females. The females respond with a glow of their own, about two seconds later.

🐜 On October 11, 1492, Columbus's crew aboard the Santa María noticed mysterious lights. The lights may have been glowworms on one of the islands of the West Indies. The tiny lights may have helped Columbus find land.

✳ Glowworms helped in the invasion of Normandy in World War II. No lights could be used. The flashing signals of glowworms gave Army jeep drivers some idea of where the road was.

✳ In some countries, men wear net bags full of fireflies tied to their ankles as home-made flashlights, and girls wear glowworms in their hair for decoration. Some Japanese gardens glow with firefly lanterns.

✳ Carbuncle beetles of Puerto Rico give off the brightest light of any animal known. One or two in a jar can provide enough light for reading a newspaper.

✳ If a June bug lands on its back it can die unless it is turned upright again.

✳ The kidnap beetle hides in ant tunnels. When an ant goes by carrying larvae, the beetle snatches the larvae out of the ant's jaws and runs away with it.

✳ The powder post beetle leaves a little trail of powdery sawdust behind when it bores holes in wood. Antique dealers try to imitate the look of these holes when they sell "old" furniture.

※ Dung beetles roll fresh dung into balls. They lay their eggs in a hole in the ball, and when the eggs hatch, the larvae eat their way through the dung.

※ The scarab, held sacred by ancient Egyptians, is a dung beetle.

※ Australian cattle farmers imported dung beetles when the droppings of 30 million cattle began to ruin their land. The problem soon disappeared.

※ The female giant water bug chases the male. When she catches him, she lays her eggs on his back, and he must carry them around until they hatch.

🐜 The world's heaviest bug is the goliath beetle, which weighs about a quarter of a pound. It is able to peel a banana.

🐜 African children play with goliath beetles, which make a whirring noise. They catch the beetle, tie a string to it, and fly it around their heads.

🐜 A leaf-eating weevil of Honolulu, Hawaii, carries small gardens on its back. The gardens are so complete that there are even animals, such as mites, living among the plants.

🐜 A male weevil sometimes has to pry the female loose when her snout gets stuck in a hole.

🐜 Whirligig beetles have eyes that are divided, which allows them to see above and below water at the same time. They are also unsinkable, because the upper part of their body surface is water-repellent.

🐜 Whirligig beetles give off an odor that smells like ripe apples. In some parts of the country they are called "penny bugs," because if you put them under your pillow at night there will be a "scent" there the next morning.

TRUE BUGS

ORDER: HEMIPTERA

🐜 Technically, the only true bug is one which pierces its victim with a sharp beak and sucks out the victim's juices.

🐜 The word "bug" was originally coined for the bed bug, which probably arrived in North America with the early explorers. Although the bite is as painful as those from most biting bugs, it does no real damage and does not transmit any disease.

The bed bug is descended from an ancestor that lived in caves and fed on the blood of bats. When people started living in caves, the bug discovered them by accident.

Assassin bugs were kept in olden times by the emirs and shahs of Central Asia for the express purpose of torturing prisoners. In 1842, Nuzaffer ed-Din, the emir of Bokhara, threw two British prisoners into a bug pit. He left them there for several months, then had them executed.

✳ The water strider is sometimes called the Jesus bug because it walks on the surface of the water. It uses the surface tension of the water to stay afloat. It rows and steers with its long middle and hind legs, which are about as thick as a horse hair. With its shorter front legs, the water strider catches prey floating by.

✳ Several species of water strider live on salt water. Some actually live out on the open seas of the Pacific, Indian, and Atlantic oceans.

✳ The backswimmer actually does the backstroke when it swims. When it is on its back in the water, its wings come together and form a kind of keel, which keeps it from turning over.

BUTTERFLIES & MOTHS
ORDER: LEPIDOPTERA

Butterflies are great sunbathers. They get their energy from solar heat, so they bask in the sun all day to soak up all the heat they need to help them fly.

Every year, millions of monarch butterflies fly to a small area in Pacific Grove, California, from their homes in Alaska and

Canada. They rest in one place called Butterfly Park. The town is so proud of their annual visitors that a fine of $500 has been imposed for killing one of the butterflies.

🐜 A hundred monarch butterflies weigh about an ounce.

🐜 Some butterflies taste bad and are not eaten by birds or lizards. Other butter-flies mimic the color and pattern of the bad-tasting butterflies, so they will not be eaten either.

🐜 The hairstreak butterfly has a "dummy" head on its wings, and moves false antennae to confuse its enemies. A South American variety flies the wrong way to puzzle its enemies.

🐜 Because some butterflies land facing the sun, they cast no shadow when their wings are folded. That makes it difficult for an enemy to see them.

🐜 Butterflies travel by day and rest at night. They rest with their wings pointing up. Moths usually fly only at night. They keep their wings spread out.

❊ Clothes moths were brought to America in the woolen garments worn by the Pilgrims.

❊ The great owlet moth of Central and South America has the largest wingspan of any moth: 14 to 17 inches.

❊ Some moths play dead when a bat is coming after them. They fold their wings and drop to the earth.

※ Skippers are usually regarded as butterflies because of their colorful appearance, but they are actually moths.

※ The male gypsy moth can tell if a female of its own species is anywhere within seven miles.

※ The gypsy moth, now a major pest, was imported from France in 1869 by a Medford, Massachusetts, naturalist. He had hoped to cross them with the American silk moth and create a hardy, thread-making caterpillar.

🐜 The sphinx moth has to do warm-ups in cool weather in order to fly. It hangs onto tree bark and makes its wings vibrate.

🐜 Caterpillars never mate. They can only produce off-spring when they are in their mature form as butterflies or moths.

🐜 Only moth caterpillars spin cocoons. Butterfly caterpillars grow a hard skin called a chrysalis, after they attach themselves to twigs.

🐜 Woolly bear caterpillars, black at both ends and brown in the middle, are believed by some people to predict the weather—the longer the middle, the longer the winter.

※ Some caterpillars live in large bunches. If one is disturbed, it raises its head and snaps back and forth. As it hits another caterpillar, that one begins snapping. Soon the whole bunch of caterpillars is snapping, which scares off birds that might eat them.

※ When the puss moth caterpillar is threatened, it vomits.

※ The silver-spotted skipper caterpillar sews the edges of leaves together to make an apartment with several rooms. Inside, the caterpillar goes into one of the rooms and molts, or slips out of its skin. Then it curls up to sleep until it awakens as a mature moth.

🐜 A caterpillar may sample a hundred different leaves before it settles down to eat one.

🐜 The elephant hawkmoth caterpillar of Europe has eye spots on its body. When it is threatened, it pulls in its head and the false "eyes" appear, making it look like the head of a snake.

✻ The Mexican jumping bean is actually the caterpillar or larva of a small bean moth. It lives inside the bean shell, and as it grows, it twists and turns, making the bean "jump."

✻ Silkworms are not really worms. They are caterpillars—the larvae of the Bombyx mori moth.

✻ Silk was discovered by the Chinese. For hundreds of years, the secret of silk was a closely guarded secret. A person could be put to death for giving the secret away.

🐜 It takes 1,500 to 2,500 silkworm cocoons to make one pound of silk.

🐜 Silkworms are finicky eaters. They prefer mulberry leaves and will eat nothing else unless they don't have a choice.

🐜 For many centuries, silk has been used in many different ways. Surgeons have used silk to replace damaged arteries in humans. It was used to straighten the teeth of an Italian woman. The kite used by Benjamin Franklin in his experiments with electricity was made of silk.

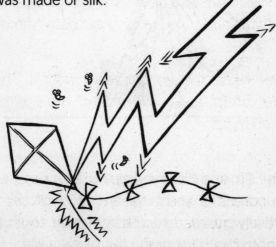

🐜 According to ancient Chinese custom, the attendant who raises silkworms, called the "silkworm mother," must not smell bad. She is not allowed to eat or touch chicory, a plant with a strong taste and smell.

🐜 Silkworm moths have adapted so thoroughly to human environments that they are no longer able to fly.

🐜 In India, women traditionally wear silk when they are married. It is a sign of respect to cover the corpse of a Hindu with silk. A silk kimono, worn in Japan, might take the work of 3,000 worms.

CICADAS
ORDER: HOMOPTERA

Cicadas live in the ground for seventeen years, but when they come out, they live for only a week. They mate and hatch eggs, and their tiny offspring disappear into the ground for the next seventeen years.

✳ Once in a while, so many cicadas emerge in the same year that thousands of their shedded skins are left behind. The skins can be spotted clinging to the trees that the cicadas last climbed to molt.

✳ The Greeks loved cicadas and kept them in cages to hear their songs. Women wore images of them in their hair. They have even appeared in their stories.

COCKROACHES
ORDER: DICTYOPTERA

🪳 Cockroaches have been around for at least 300 million years. Fossils show that they were once nearly a foot long.

🪳 Cockroaches are tough. They can live for several weeks with their heads removed before they starve to death. They can be frozen and still walk away after they thaw.

They can even live through 100 times as much radiation as humans can.

 Cockroaches will eat almost anything. Some live inside the backs of TV sets and never come out. They live on glue, insulation, and other components inside the TV set. Sometimes, they eat through the insulation, causing a short circuit.

CRICKETS, GRASSHOPPERS, & KATYDIDS
ORDER: ORTHOPTERA

※ Some people believe that crickets can forecast the temperature—count the number of chirps a cricket makes in 15 seconds and add 40.

※ The name "cricket" comes from the old French verb "craquer," which means "to creak" or "to click."

※ In Asian cultures, crickets are kept as pets in tiny bamboo cages so their owners can enjoy their singing.

🐜 A cricket singing near the fireplace is supposed to mean good luck.

🐜 Experts found that hopping grasshoppers grow wings and change into flying grasshoppers when it is extremely hot and they are extremely hungry.

🐜 A jet black grasshopper of Australia turns sky blue when the sun comes up in the morning.

✹ Some grasshoppers can "throw their voices" by adjusting the angle of their forewings. This confuses predators.

✹ In Germany, people once bought little cardboard "hopper houses" in which to keep a pet katydid.

✹ The katydid repeats its call about 50 million times in one summer.

DRAGONFLIES & DAMSELFLIES
ORDER: ODONATA

※ The largest insect ever to inhabit the earth was a dragonfly. It lived 250 million years ago, and experts believe its wings spread up to 4 feet across.

※ The dragonfly has six legs but never walks. It uses four of its legs like a little basket to hold food that it gathers when it flies, scooping up tiny, flying insects with the other two legs.

✳ People once believed that dragonflies, also called "darning needles" and "devil doctors," would sew up your ears or lips or even your eyelids.

✳ While the female damselfly lays her eggs below the water surface, the male hangs onto her by the neck. If he lets go, she drowns.

FLEAS
ORDER: SIPHONAPTERA

🦟 The tiny flea has caused millions of deaths. In the 14th century, nearly a quarter of the population of Europe was wiped out by bubonic plague, a disease spread by fleas.

🦟 In an agricultural document called the *Geoponica*, the Greeks advised that people who found themselves in a flea-infested area should cry "Ouch! Ouch!" and no flea would touch them.

✹ The ancient Romans thought fleas came alive from dust or dirt. Later, scholars believed they grew out of pigeon poop, goat urine, and beads of sweat dropped from the brows of slaves.

✹ The Romans had a cure for removing fleas from the ears. A patient was tied to a plank supported at its middle, like a seesaw. The patient was tilted, with the affected ear on the downside, extending beyond the end of the plank. Then the upper end of the plank at the patient's feet was struck with a mallet, and the ear was so jarred that the flea dropped out.

🦟 Christina, queen of Sweden in the 17th century, enjoyed paying back those who brought torment to humans. For amusement, she had made to order a 4-inch-long gun, which she used only for flea executions. The gun is exhibited today in the arsenal at Stockholm.

🦟 If a human could imitate the flea in proportion to its body size, he could do a standing broad jump of a quarter of a mile.

🦟 Nuns in Mexico once entertained themselves by dressing fleas in elaborate costumes. Then they sold the fleas as souvenirs.

🦟 The English were the first to exhibit fleas dressed up and involved in amazing activities, like pulling carts or dancing. These "flea circuses" became a regular entertainment at fairs and markets. The most famous flea circus was owned by Britain's Len Tomlin, who harnessed fleas by fine silver wires, using a jeweler's tweezers and eyeglass. The captive fleas would walk a tightrope, juggle, and cycle.

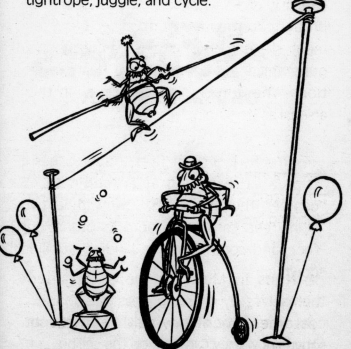

FLIES & MOSQUITOES
ORDER: DIPTERA

🐜 The fly is a stunt flyer. It approaches a spot on the ceiling at an angle of 45 degrees. Then it touches down with its two front feet, cartwheels onto its other four feet, and completes the landing—upside down.

🐜 Flies have sticky pads on their feet. That's how they can walk on the ceiling.

✳ The average housefly lives for only two to three weeks, but it might leave more than 5 trillion descendants in a single year.

✳ It's hard to swat a fly because the hairs on its legs are very sensitive to changes in air pressure. That's why fly swatters are made with holes in them—to reduce the air pressure.

✳ The housefly can locate sugar with its feet, which are 10 million times more sensitive than the human tongue.

✳ Maggots, the larvae of flies, were used in primitive medicine. Placed on wounds, they ate dead tissue, allowing the wound to heal more quickly.

✳ The eye of a fly has 28,000 lenses that allow it to see 360 degrees around itself.

✳ In the Waitomo Caves of New Zealand, tiny worms—the larvae of small flies—give off a tiny glow that draws prey to them. In the dark depths of the caves, they look like stars in a night sky.

✳ Robber flies impersonate bumblebees. Although they are flies, they look and act like bumble-bees. They even hang around gardens and flowers, looking so much like bees that birds leave them alone.

✳ How fast the blackfly makes its start in life determines whether it lives or dies. It starts out as a larva and then becomes a pupa in the rapids of a stream. The new blackfly hatches in an air bubble in the rushing water of the stream. When the bubble bursts, the fly must spring into the air. If it takes too long, it will drown in the rushing waters.

✳ Domestic animals have been killed by blackflies. At times, so many blackflies come out at once that they get into the noses, mouths, and breathing passages of animals, which suffocates them.

✹ When Hessian soldiers arrived in the colonies to help the British during the American Revolution, the tiny gnat came along in their straw mattresses. It has been a major problem for American wheat farmers ever since.

✹ The word "mosquito" comes from the Spanish and Portuguese word for "little fly."

✹ Once a female mosquito mates, it has no desire ever to mate again.

✳️ Only the female mosquito is able to bite. She needs that little bit of blood for her eggs to develop.

✳️ A wingless mosquito is the biggest land animal on Antarctica.

✳️ The mosquito has caused more people to die than all the wars in history. Certain species carry the germ that causes malaria.

PRAYING MANTISES
ORDER: ORTHOPTERA

🐜 The praying mantis is not really praying. Its front legs are folded and ready to snap open when it wants to grab another insect for a meal.

🐜 A praying mantis may eat a fellow mantis—or even a part of its own body.

🐜 Although the praying mantis feeds on all kinds of insects, it will never eat an ant. The mantis is afraid of even the tiniest ant.

🐜 The praying mantis can strike its prey in about 60 thousandths of a second.

🐜 In Japan, mantises are kept on long threads, like leashes, to act as living insect-catchers in a house.

🐜 Mantises have been kept as pets. One man took his pet mantis on business trips to New York. He carried the mantis in his briefcase.

SPIDERS, SCORPIONS, & TICKS
ORDER: ARANEIDA

🕷 There are several ways to tell a spider from an insect. One is to count the legs. All spiders have eight legs, while insects have only six. Also, spiders have only two body segments, while insects have three. And spiders never, ever have wings, but many insects do.

🕷 A spider of one species cannot mate with one of another species.

 Spiders begin life by "ballooning." They stand on tiptoe, let out some silk, and wait for a breeze to lift them into the air. They float on air currents on silk threads, sometimes for hundreds of miles, until they land in a spot where they can begin their lives.

🕷 The daddy longlegs is also known as the shepherd spider because for centuries it was believed that it could help find lost cows. Shepherds were simply to follow the direction in which the daddy longlegs' second pair of legs was pointing.

🕷 The venom of the black widow spider is fifteen times more powerful than that of the rattlesnake. The amount of venom it can inject is so small, however, that few people die after being bitten.

🕷 The highest land animal on earth is the small black attid spider. It lives at an altitude of 22,000 feet on Mount Everest, the peak of the Himalayas. Wild sheep and mountain goats in the Himalayan Mountains live only as far up as 17,000 feet.

🕷 After mating, the female spider often eats the male, but some males have found clever ways to avoid being killed. One wraps the female in silk so he has time to escape after mating. Another lassoes its mate, then ties down her feet before he mates. A third presents the female with a present, gift-wrapped. While she is busy unwrapping it, he mates with her and makes his getaway. Still another tugs at the female's web and strokes or pats her until she is hypnotized.

✳ In the Middle Ages, Europeans believed that the bite of a wolf spider, or tarantula, was fatal. If they thought they had been bitten, they danced wildly for hours to rid their bodies of the poison. In Italy, this "dance" became known as the *tarantella*.

✳ A tarantula has never been known to kill a human.

✳ Most web-weaving spiders have poor eyesight. They know when an insect has landed in a web by the vibration they feel.

✳ All spider webs are designed to trap insects for food.

✳ A tropical spider builds a tiny web, about an inch in diameter, and throws it over passing insects like a net.

✳ Not all spiders spin webs. Some spiders pounce on their victims instead of using a web to trap them.

✳ It's not clear why spiders do not get stuck in their own webs. Possibly, their legs are covered with an oily substance that won't stick to the web material.

✱ In many species, if a spider's leg is missing, it will grow a new one during the molting process.

✱ The aquatic spider of Europe and Asia builds a bell-shaped web under water, filling it with air bubbles. Then it lives in the bell, preying on aquatic species for its food supply. It replenishes its air supply as needed.

✱ Spiders can't chew or swallow solid food. They inject their victims with a fluid that turns the victims' insides into a kind of soup. Then the spiders suck it up.

🕷 In the Near East, a spider is considered a sign of good luck. Newlyweds often find one placed in their bed.

🕷 When a victim is too big to handle, the bird-eating spider of the Amazon jungle throws poisonous hairs at its victim. It has also been known to place these poisonous hairs in the nests of baby birds.

🕷 The silk spun by spiders is so strong that people in tropical countries use its threads to make nets for fishing. Strands of it have been used as cross hairs in telescopes, binoculars, microscopes, and gunsights.

🕷 A wolf spider mom takes her offspring for walks, piling about two hundred of them on her back. If any fall off, she waits until they climb back up her legs and then she continues the walk.

🕷 Certain spiders mimic ants. They have a small waist like ants and walk on three pair of their legs, instead of four. They hold the fourth pair of legs forward to look like antennae.

✳ The spider has been used as a model for robots that can walk across uneven terrain, such as the land on the moon or other planets.

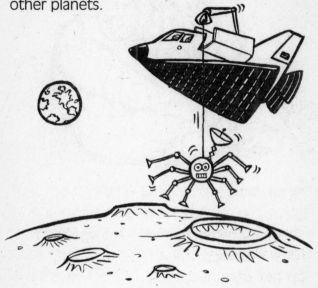

✳ Most scorpion stings are not serious. The exception is the sting from the Durango scorpion of Mexico, which can be fatal to humans.

✳ Scorpions walk forward at a normal pace but move like lightning when they go backward.

🐜 In some parts of the African country of Sudan, the remedy for a scorpion sting is to rub the affected area with the charred toe-nail of a baboon.

🐜 A tick is the size of a grain of rice when it is empty. Once it attaches itself to an animal and fills up with blood, it can grow as big as a marble.

TERMITES
ORDER: ISOPTERA

🐜 The termite civilization is at least 30 million years old, which makes it the oldest civilization on earth. Termites are the only insects that have a king rather than a queen.

🐜 Termite mounds are like insect skyscrapers. Some in Africa and Australia are 15 to 20 feet high and 12 feet wide. They can be built out of sand, clay, or sawdust, mixed with saliva. Some clay nests are so hard they can only be broken with a pickax. Early Spanish settlers in Brazil hollowed out the clay nests and used them as ovens.

※ Compass termites build tall, skinny nests that are 8 to 10 feet high and shaped like the head of an ax, with the narrow ends always pointing north and south.

※ When something disturbs a termite nest, soldier termites bang their heads or bodies against the tunnel walls. Others along the tunnel hear it and do the same. Soon, every termite in the nest has heard the alarm.

🐜 Termites eat wood, but cannot digest it without certain bacteria or protozoa in their systems. If the bacteria were removed, termites would continue to eat wood, but they would starve to death.

🐜 A newborn termite has no protozoa. Some scientists believe it gets some by licking its neighbors like lollipops.

🐜 Termites are not members of the ant family, as most people assume, but are related to cockroaches.

Termites cannot stand strong light. A few species carry little paperlike parasols for shade when they come up out of the ground.

CLOSE KIN & DISTANT COUSINS

🐜 Earthworms (Order: *Nematoda*) "plow" the soil for farmers. As the worms wriggle under the ground, they not only loosen the soil, which helps circulate air through it, but they carry new, rich soil up to the surface.

🐜 There are about 50,000 earthworms in an acre of soil.

🐜 A ton of earthworms can turn a ton of organic garbage into good soil. The worms absorb all organic matter in the soil and cast it out along with a dose of digestive fluid. The castings are rich in nutrients and act as fertilizer.

🐜 Aristotle, a famous Greek philosopher, called the earthworm the "intestines of the earth."

🐜 Earthworms in Australia grow to be 11 feet long. If they stretch out, they can be 21 feet long.

❋ There are worms in the Himalayas, vaguely related to earthworms, that commit suicide every year by casting off their own heads. Scientists believe that these odd worms lay their eggs with such violent movements that the front parts of their bodies are flung off.

❋ The walking stick (Order: **Phasmatodea**) is the longest insect in the world. It can grow to be 13 inches long.

❋ A master of mimicry, the walking stick looks exactly like the twig it lives on.

The larva of the caddisfly (Order: *Trichoptera*) makes a little tube out of sticks or sand and lives in it under water. As it crawls along the bottom, it pulls its little tube house along with it.

The male mayfly (Order: *Ephemeroptera*) does not eat and does not even have a mouth. Once it emerges from the water, it lives for only two hours. All it can do is mate and die. The female lives a little bit longer, about four hours, so she can lay her eggs.

🐜 The number of legs on a centipede (Order: **Scutigeromorpha**) varies between 13 and 181 pairs. It has a pair of legs for each segment of its body.

🐜 There are centipedes that can keep up with a person who is taking a leisurely walk.

🐜 Ribbon worms (Order: **Rhynchocoela**), which can grow to be 90 feet long, tie themselves hopelessly into knots.

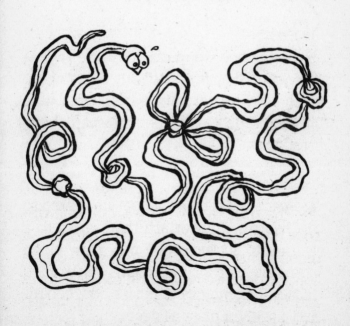

🐜 Ribbon worms build their houses from the slime of their own bodies.

🐜 The ribbon worm can spear prey with a "harpoon" that it shoots out of its brain. After a tiny water animal is speared, it is brought in by a long string attached to the harpoon.

🐜 Leeches (Order: **Annelida**) are related to earthworms. They attach themselves to a victim with suckers. Then they draw blood from the victim. Physicians have used leeches for centuries to draw blood, considered a cure for many ailments.

🐜 In the Middle Ages, it was thought that a cure for indigestion was to place twenty to thirty leeches around the stomach. A high fever was treated with a band of leeches around the head.

🐜 There was such a demand for leeches in late 18th century France that peasants were sent into bogs and marshes to collect them. The leeches clung to the peasants' legs as they emerged from the water.

🐜 The saliva of leeches contains a substance called *hirudin*, which slows down the clotting of blood. It was once used in surgery.

🐜 Boxers with black eyes still sometimes use leeches to drain the bruised blood from around their eyes.

🐜 The tapeworm (Order: **Annelida**) lives inside the intestines of larger animals, including humans. It lives off the food that passes through the body during digestion.

GLOSSARY

antennae—extensions on an insect's head that help the insect feel or smell

class—a group of related orders

cocoon—a protective case that contains an insect before it is fully grown

colony—a place where many members of a species, such as ants or termites, live

larva—the earliest stage in the development of an insect

maggots—the larvae of flies

molting—shedding an outer covering

nectar—a sweet liquid that comes from plants

offspring—the young that are produced by any creature

order—a group that has similar characteristics, such as straight wings or chewing mouths

pheromones—a substance given off by an insect to attract a mate

pollen—a fine powder in plants that bees collect to make into honey

pollinate—transferring pollen from one plant to another

prey—an animal taken as food

protozoa—tiny organisms

queen—the only female in a colony that can be a mother

royal jelly—a rich food that is fed to the queen bee and baby bees

soldier—a worker insect with an exceptionally large head and jaws

species—a basic unit of classification in the animal and plant kingdoms

thorax—the middle segment of an insect's body

venom—poison

workers—members of an insect colony that do all the work

INDEX